Original title:
Breezes of the Southern Isles

Copyright © 2025 Creative Arts Management OÜ
All rights reserved.

Author: Aurora Sinclair
ISBN HARDBACK: 978-1-80581-701-7
ISBN PAPERBACK: 978-1-80581-228-9
ISBN EBOOK: 978-1-80581-701-7

Sounds of Silence by the Shore

The seagulls debate, squawking loud,
Crabs in a scramble, they look so proud.
A beach ball bounces, oh, what a sight,
While sunscreen slips—someone's in for a fright.

Sandcastles topple with one little shove,
A kid on a floaty, resembling a dove.
Sand in their pants, they giggle and squeal,
With shells for a snack, it's a great big meal.

Nightfall's Soft Embrace

The moon winks brightly, a shimmering tease,
While jellyfish dance, floating with ease.
A crab takes a stroll, with swagger and grace,
Only to trip on a starfish's face.

Stars overhead seem to twinkle and grin,
As owls hoot tunes, and fish dive in.
A night-time swim, lit by phosphorescent light,
Hilarity ensues with each splashy fight.

Upon Waves of Gentle Motion

Surfboards tumble in a salty embrace,
One surfer's a legend, though he's lost in space.
A dolphin pops up, with a wink and a flip,
While a kite surfer sways, barely holding a grip.

The sun wears its shades, the sand's at a trot,
As beachgoers scatter, all chasing their hot.
A game of beach volleyball goes awry,
With a ball to the face, oh me, oh my!

Echoing Footsteps on Forgotten Trails

Barefoot adventurers take the lost path,
Finding odd treasures, and giggling with glee.
An old pair of sandals? Just look at that mess!
Who knew that a flip-flop could bring such distress?

A turtle plays hide and seek in the brush,
While tourists snap pics, in a hasty rush.
Each thump of their footsteps, a dance to behold,
As laughter erupts; life never gets old.

Chasing Distant Horizons

With laughter loud, we sprint along,
A race with seagulls, what could go wrong?
The sun's too bright, the sand's too hot,
Our flip-flops fly; we're losing the plot.

A crab waves claws, we shout in glee,
"Look at him dance!" Oh, what a sight to see!
We trip, we laugh, we tumble down,
The fish nearby just wear a frown.

Notes from the Glistening Cove

A message in a bottle, oh what a catch,
Turns out it's just a potato, not a match!
We giggle and snicker, what a fine tease,
The ocean's humor always aims to please.

The waves crash in like they own the show,
"Please stop crashing!" we tell them, but they don't know!

We build up castles, they knock them down,
Swearing revenge, we wear our best frowns.

Shadows of Clouds Over the Bay

Cloud sculptures float, a lion appears,
We roar at each other, contagious our cheers!
Then a cat rolls by, with shadows we play,
"You're not a lion!" we giggle away.

A rogue gust whispers, our hats take flight,
Chasing them down, it's quite the sight!
Fishermen chuckle, they sip with grace,
While we perform a rather wild chase.

Hushed Conversations with the Sea

The tide whispers secrets, a sly little chap,
It tickles our toes and gives us a slap.
"Did you hear that?" someone shouts in surprise,
The sea just chuckles with its oceanic sighs.

Starfish gossip under the shimmering sky,
"Did you hear about the crab?" Oh me, oh my!
We laugh till we cry, what folly we've found,
The waves just roll on, they've heard it around.

Echoes of Island Laughter

In the shade where coconuts sway,
A parrot jokes, brightening the day.
Monkeys chuckle, swinging 'round,
As a slippery crab looks so profound.

Tourists stumble, with drinks in hand,
A flip-flop goes flying, that was not planned!
The sun smiles down, a jester's show,
With sandy feet, they dance in a row.

Tides of Tranquil Harmony

The waves whisper secrets to the sand,
As a fish laughs, doing its best handstand.
Shells giggle, sparkling under the sun,
While a lazy dog barks just for fun.

Hammock swings in a lazy bliss,
A friendly seagull steals a kiss.
With warm sunbeams and laughter bright,
We sip cool drinks, all feels just right.

Gentle Winds Over Coral Reefs

Coral crabs tiptoe with a flair,
While bubbles burst, causing quite the scare.
A swordfish dons a dashing hat,
As dolphins giggle, how silly is that!

Underwater parties, a sight to see,
With fish in tuxedos dancing with glee.
The ocean sings, a bubbly delight,
As we all join in, feeling so light.

Vibrations of Paradise Air

The breeze carries tinkles of a bell,
As palm trees sway, they cast a spell.
Starfruits chuckle, hanging from high,
While iguanas sunbathe, oh my, oh my!

Picnic antics on a checkered cloth,
A sandwich floats by, what a froth!
Laughter erupts, echoes through the sky,
In this endless playground, joy will fly.

Mornings Filled with Tropical Light

The roosters sing, a morning tune,
With coffee spills and toasty croon.
Island strolls, we trip and slide,
In flip-flops lost, with grins so wide.

A parrot squawks, we blink and laugh,
As surfboards tumble, oh what a gaffe!
The sun peeks in, the palms now sway,
We dance like fish, in bright array.

Flavors of the Ocean's Caress

Shark with shades, he swims past me,
Winks a fin, says, 'Join my spree!'
Pineapple juice spills on my toes,
While jellyfish tease with ticklish woes.

Tacos fly, a seagull's theft,
'Leave some for me!' a voice bereft.
Laughter blends with the ocean's roar,
As we feast and tumble on the shore.

Joy Beneath the Mango Trees

Mangoes drop with a juicy plop,
We scramble fast—not a single stop!
A playful breeze makes us spin and twirl,
As the world around us starts to whirl.

Friends gather round, with sticky hands,
Sharing stories like shifting sands.
The laughter rings, like coconut shells,
Under their shade, where bliss compels.

Twilight's Embrace in Sandy Nooks

Sunset spills its golden hues,
As we cast shadows, in playful views.
Giggles echo, a crab in retreat,
Bumps my toe, it's quite the feat!

With glowsticks glowing, we'll dance all night,
Under the stars, the waves invite.
As laughter fades, the crickets hum,
In sandy nooks, our hearts feel young.

Swaying Palms and Ocean's Kiss

Palm trees dance with flair,
While seagulls steal the snacks,
Someone's hat flies through the air,
As laughter fills the cracks.

The sun dips low, it winks,
A crab scuttles with great speed,
Caught in a game of jinx,
Chasing folks, oh what a breed!

Sand's a drink for all the toes,
A flip-flop's thrown, it lands with flair,
Watch out for the beachside pose,
Where dignity goes to declare!

As the waves tickle the shore,
A kite gets tangled in a mess,
With friends, there's always more,
Just don't forget the sunscreen stress!

Secrets in the Salted Air

The ocean whispers, "Hey there!"
In its salty, funny ways,
With fish that love to stare,
And shells that sing in sunlit rays.

Underneath a coconut tree,
A monkey makes a grand old fuss,
He flings a coconut with glee,
And we just laugh, no need to rush!

Seagulls squawk their loudest tales,
Of crabs playing hide-and-seek,
While the sunset slowly pales,
And everyone's too tired to speak.

What mysteries the tide may hold,
As the night brings stars to call,
With laughter new and tales retold,
Under the moon, we cherish all!

Dreams Carried on the Wind

Windswept hair and goofy grins,
As laughter wraps around us tight,
With dreams of seashells, smiles, and sins,
We chase the fading daylight bright.

A surfboard tossed up in the air,
Crashes down with a clueless thud,
The crowd erupts in carefree flare,
"Is that supposed to be a 'stud'?"

Beach towels flying like great kites,
With sandwiches that peel and flop,
Each picnic turns into delights,
As chips and dip tumble, plop!

And as we glide into the night,
The stars above twinkle and tease,
Whispered plans of future flight,
On winds that carry our unease.

Sunlit Shores and Feathered Friends

On sunlit shores, where laughter sprawls,
Birds steal snacks with cheeky flair,
Each seagull knows the fun that calls,
And dives to snatch what's in the air.

The children chase their flying hats,
While sandcastles tumble and fall,
A crab plays tag with giggling cats,
Oh, what a merry, silly sprawl!

The sun smiles wide, glowing bright,
As sand gets stuck to sticky skin,
We bake beneath its golden light,
With ice cream stands, our favored kin.

And when the stars pop out to play,
We'll share our stories, loud and free,
With feathered friends who lead the way,
To silly dreams and salty glee!

Petals on the Water's Surface

Petals dance on water, they sip the sun,
A drunken little boat thinks it's a ton.
Fish gossip below, sharing tales of old,
While turtles wear shades, getting sun-kissed gold.

Frivolous frogs croak like they're in a show,
The snails start a race, but they move too slow.
A duck joins the fun, in a loud, quacky voice,
Even the lily gets up—it's time to rejoice!

Waves giggle and splash, the sea's in a prank,
Shells whispering secrets, as they sit on the bank.
A crab with a crown thinks he's our new king,
But he forgets his throne is a discarded ring.

As clouds tickle skies, with laughter, they roam,
Stars peek from above, saying, "Is this your home?"
In this floaty circus, where joy finds its way,
The petals keep swirling, it's a happy ballet.

Shadows of Palm Trees at Dusk

Tall palms play charades, as shadows unfold,
A raccoon pops out, his secrets retold.
The coconuts chuckle, hanging way up high,
While squirrels on stilts wave and dance while they fly.

A lizard struts by, strutting with all his flair,
He drops his cool shades, oh, what a despair!
But he flips with a grin, saying, "No sweat!"
Making folks laugh, it's the best trick yet.

Twilight confetti, the sky's painted beige,
Moon winks at the stars, it's a fun little stage.
While breezy jokes travel, like whispers on wings,
The shadows giggle softly, oh what joy it brings!

Yet bats with bad jokes, appear out of the blue,
They hang upside down, sharing puns just for you.
The palms roll their eyes, full of leafy delight,
As dusk wraps the island, with laughter so bright.

Luminescence of Midnight Waters

In midnight's embrace, the waters will glow,
Jellyfish float by, throwing a light show.
They wiggle and giggle, with each wave they make,
Turning dark into disco, for the ocean's sake.

Moonfish in tuxedos, swim with such flair,
They twirl and they leap, without a single care.
While starfish are judges, with scores in their fins,
Saying, "You missed a beat—let's try again, twins!"

Crabs in a chorus, croon sweet serenades,
Their giddy pinch dance, brightening the shades.
The wave hops along, in rhythm it prances,
As seaweed enthusiasts join in with glances.

But when the night grins and starts to fade,
The party wraps up, a grand escapade.
With shells raising toasts, and laughter in tow,
These glowing waters know how to throw a show.

Embrace of the Monsoon's Breath

A raincloud rolls in, with a mischievous grin,
Dancing on rooftops, it loves to begin.
Puddles are puddles, but they're also for splashes,
Kids in their galoshes, like fishes, make dashes.

Umbrellas fly high, a circus of sorts,
As laughter erupts at their comical sports.
The raindrops compete in a slippery race,
While frogs chant their verses—you're in our space!

A kite gets swept up, oh don't be afraid,
It swoops like a bird, in joyful cascade.
The trees sway and shimmy, embracing the storm,
While wind takes a bow, in its wild, swirling form.

As the clouds fade away, the sun makes a scene,
Leaving everyone drenched, yet feeling quite clean.
With a wink and a nod, the monsoon departs,
Leaving wet, happy smiles in all of our hearts.

Sails Against a Vermilion Sky

Sailing high on a candy cloud,
We laugh at fish that dance and bow.
The sun is a grill, the sea a fry,
How the seagulls squawk, we'll show them how!

With laughter bubbling like tropical stew,
The captain's hat sails right off his head.
A parrot squawks, "I'll take it too!"
While we recount tales of wobbly bread!

The horizon blushes, a cheeky grin,
We toast to a life of funny mishaps.
In waves of joy, we just dive in,
As our boat hugs the shore, no time for maps!

With a belly full of laughter, we glide,
The sea's a jester, a playful mime.
Each wave a chuckle as we all ride,
And we find our rhythm, every silly rhyme.

Isles of Serenity and Solitude

In islands where coconuts wear a smile,
We trip on sand, oh, what a style!
Palm trees gossip, swaying, swirling,
While crabs play tag, they're all unfurling!

A hammock naps under a lazy sun,
We're trading stories, laughter, and fun.
The waves send jokes in splashes and roar,
As the sun does a shimmy on the sandy floor!

Starfish hold secret parades at night,
While we wear sunglasses that don't fit quite right.
In this realm of giggles and soft ocean sighs,
We ponder if pineapple really belongs on pies!

As dusk paints the sky with rambunctious hues,
We dance with shadows, with laughter we cruise.
In these cheerful isles, we're never alone,
Because every wave's a friend we've known!

Woven Paths of Driftwood

Driftwood wanderers, we stroll in a line,
Trading secrets with each piece of twine.
With sand in our shoes and stars in our hair,
We weave tales from shells with the utmost flair!

A turtle in glasses gives us a wink,
While jellyfish float with a classier blink.
Is this a beach or a party affair?
As crabs critique our dance moves with care!

We build a fortress, a castle of fun,
But the tide has a joke, and it's coming undone.
Laughter erupts as our dreams slip away,
Turning our castles to splashes in play!

Nature's own circus, it spins and it twirls,
With antics that twist as the tide softly swirls.
Our pathways of driftwood lead to delight,
In the humorous dance of the deepening night!

Whirling Colors at Sunset

The sun's taking bows, a dramatic retreat,
As clouds wear ochre, a colorful sheet.
We laugh at the colors as they spin and sway,
Painting the sky in a glorious display!

A flamingo joints our team with flair,
Balancing dreams on its thin, pink pair.
As laughter erupts in the evening glow,
It shows us who wiggles the best, oh no!

We chase the shadows, a merry parade,
With a disco ball sun that won't ever fade.
The ocean whispers its secret giggle,
While we all trip to the sunset's jiggle!

In a whirl of colors, we shout out our joys,
While chasing the twilight like playful toys.
The night wraps us up in its twinkling embrace,
As we spin through the laughter, a mischievous race.

Glimmers of the Day's Last Breath

The sun dips low, a golden disk,
As seagulls squawk, and people risk.
With laughter loud, we dance and sway,
In twilight's glow, we play all day.

The drinks are spiced, they tickle our nose,
While sand clings tight to our toes.
A mischief breeze grabs at my hat,
And off it goes, that cheeky brat!

With cocoanuts bobbing by the shore,
We sip and laugh; we always want more.
A flip-flop flings, over goes a friend,
In silliness, this night just won't end!

As stars peek through, like confetti bright,
We revel deep into the night.
Glimmers fade, yet laughter stays,
In this, our paradise, we share our plays.

Pools of Serenity by the Cliff's Edge

Atop the cliffs, a pool so clear,
Where sunken dreams and laughs appear.
The fish wave fins, they call us down,
While we play kings and wear a crown.

With plunges loud, we make a splash,
The water flies in swirling flash.
But slippery rocks, they test our grace,
A friendly tumble, what a case!

We laugh and roll, our worries drown,
A slip, a slide, the best of clowns.
With giggles echoing all around,
We find true joy; it knows no bound.

As sunsets paint the cliffs in hues,
We toast our fun, drink in the views.
Tomorrow calls; we will return,
To dance with joy, let spirits burn.

Reflections of a Distant Horizon

With flip-flops squeaking on the sand,
We chase the waves, a merry band.
The horizon laughs, a distant tease,
And who knows where? The breeze agrees!

A crab sits proud, its shell so grand,
We tiptoe close, it's not a fan.
With claws held high, it makes a stand,
We giggle loud, it's too well planned!

Shells drift past as if they know,
The tales of tides, the ebb and flow.
With silly faces and dance routines,
We make them smile; they're our marine queens!

As day drifts by, the sun bows low,
We wave goodbye, still riding the glow.
Tomorrow's folly, we'll recompose,
For laughter's treasure is what we chose.

The Quiet Pulse of Island Life

In island grace, the days unwind,
With roosters singing, they're not so kind.
A hammock sways, with giggles near,
The quiet pulse, we hold so dear.

When tourists come, they breathe and sigh,
Yet locals know just how to fly.
With swaying palms and fruits so sweet,
We dance through life, no need for beat!

An iguana nods, it gives its cheer,
As fish leap high, their jumps sincere.
With every phase of sun and moon,
Its pulse is fun, a joyous tune!

In evenings spent with friends so dear,
We share our stories, hearts sincere.
No fancy bars, no worldly strife,
Just a simple, quiet island life.

Tales Borne on Island Vistas

Jokes fly high with the gulls afloat,
While sunburnt tourists misplace their boat.
One sunhat flies, then another's lost,
South seas laughter, at any cost.

Palm trees wag with the monkey's tease,
As locals dance with a playful breeze.
Flip-flops lost, and someone yells,
The ocean's rhythm rings like bells.

Hammocks sway after the midday feast,
Sipping drinks with a wild, fruity beast.
Laughter echoes as crabs take a stroll,
Nature's comedy, playing its role.

In flip-flops and shorts, we dance in the sun,
Collecting each smile, this fun just begun.
With a wink and a grin, our worries take flight,
Island adventures, our hearts full of light.

Imprints in Soft, Warm Sand

Footprints sketch silly in the golden granule,
While kids bury parents, an amusing channel.
Seagulls squawk gossip, and waves sing along,
As laughter erupts like a joyful song.

Tanned toes tremble near crabs on parade,
A shell collector's bust is solidly made.
Organizing seashells can take a wrong turn,
As slippery barnacles teach us to learn.

Beach balls bounce high, like thoughts in our heads,
Family feuds waged on who wins the spreads.
Caught in a wave, someone slips and dives,
Rolling in laughter, that's how joy thrives.

Sunburned and sandy, we gather our gear,
Sharing ole tales that all come with cheer.
With buckets and spades, let silly times reign,
In soft, warm sand, we dance without pain.

Essence of Tropical Dawn

Morning sun peeks through the palm's embrace,
A coffee cup tipped, painting a mess on my face.
The rooster's crow sounds like a clown's laugh,
As we giggle through breakfast, swapping the gaffe.

Waves tickle our toes, a playful affair,
Fish tease the net, hanging light in the air.
With a wink and a splash, we dive in so quick,
Once mighty swimmers now float like a brick.

Beneath a sky blossomed bright with cheer,
Joking with locals, we sip on our beer.
As parrots squawk gossip, we join all in fun,
With a wink and a grin, every day's just begun.

Sunsets paint giggles, the horizon aglow,
Each moment a treasure, let's make sure it flows.
With candy-coated smiles, we dance till the night,
The essence of laughter, our spirits take flight.

A Canvas of Coral Dreams

Underwater laughter in colors ablaze,
Finding lost goggles while fish swim in daze.
A snorkeler coughs, spitting sea and glee,
As the clownfish point, it's a sight to see.

Coral castles hold stories from deep,
Where mermaids giggle and dolphins leap.
With each wave brushes, life sways in art,
Making a portrait right from the heart.

Flip through the ocean like pages of lore,
Where sea turtles race and the jellyfish soar.
A treasure trove story, planted in sand,
With a wink and a splash, let's make a band.

So come join the fun, paint memories wide,
On this canvas of colors, we'll take a ride.
Joking as tides bring us laughter so bright,
In a world under waves, everything feels right.

Serenade of Sunlit Shores

Sandy toes and sun-kissed noses,
Laughter bounces, a joyful roses.
Seagulls squawk for a crumb or two,
While crabs dance much like me and you.

Shells are treasures, a pirate's glee,
And flip-flops sing, oh can't you see?
The waves are ticklish, they splash and play,
As sunburnt friends shout hip-hip-hooray!

Umbrellas fight with the wind so bold,
Like old folks bickering, or so I'm told.
Yet smiles are bright, like the sun's own ray,
Here in our kingdom of sand and sway.

With ice-cream cones that start to melt,
We dance on the shore, oh what a felt.
Nothing like sunshine, friends, and fun,
With a side of laughter, we all have won!

Embrace of Coastal Dreams

Dunes like pillows, so soft and fluffy,
Jellyfish bounce, though they can be stuffy.
Seashells whisper their sandy schemes,
While we dream big by the coastal beams.

In flip-flops, we shuffle, stroll with flair,
And seagulls plot on how to snare.
A beach ball flies, with wild intent,
As laughter trails in its playful ascent.

Hats blow off like they have a mind,
Oh, there goes Dave—his hair is unlined!
But joy sticks around, right by our side,
With lemonade smiles, let's enjoy the ride!

The tide rolls in with a playful grin,
While splashes and giggles clearly begin.
Hand in hand, with our spirits ablaze,
We dance with the surf in a sun-drunk daze.

Breezy Lullabies at Dusk

The sky's a canvas, pink and blue,
While the fish plan their great escape too.
Kids run wild, their laughter's the key,
As the sun sinks low, quite carefree!

Sunscreen smeared like war paint true,
Squawking gulls give their feathery review.
Picnics sprawled like an artist's dream,
With sandwiches plotting the next big scheme.

Kites soaring high, tugging on string,
As a gentle breeze makes the sea foam sing.
The stars peek out in a twinkling jest,
While crickets play tunes that never rest.

We gather 'round with giggles and cheer,
Telling tales while the moon draws near.
With friends at our side, nothing can quell,
These laughter-filled moments, a magical spell!

Secrets of Swaying Palms

Whispers from palms that sway with style,
Palm leaves gossip—let's sit awhile.
A coconut drops, it's a splashy surprise,
While squirrels prance with mischievous eyes.

Sunhats tilted at a jaunty angle,
Mermaids giggle, their tresses all dangle.
A piña colada spills by a shore,
While flip-flops argue, 'We want more!'

The hammock sways as if sensing dreams,
While kids plot schemes with giggle-filled screams.
Each sunset's glow, a mischievous buy,
As stars sprinkle laughter across the sky.

With sunglasses on, we toast to the night,
Here's to the secrets of joyful delight.
We dance with the moon, in rhythms so rare,
As the palms join in, swaying with flair!

Isles of Enchantment and Reverie

In a land where coconuts play,
Monkeys swing in a comical way.
The sun wears sunglasses, quite a sight,
While crabs do the cha-cha, day and night.

A parrot tells jokes, full of glee,
While sea turtles chuckle near the sea.
Flip-flops dance on feet so bare,
As jellyfish giggle without a care.

Sandcastles with moats filled with soup,
Shells hold secrets, in a funny loop.
Fish wear hats, looking quite grand,
In this whimsical, sun-kissed land.

With laughter in the salty breeze,
Seagulls drop fries with practiced ease.
Mermaids giggle, their hair all a mess,
In these isles of fun, we're truly blessed.

Panoramic Dreams of Serene Shores

On shores where crabs race with flair,
Sunbathers snooze in their messy hair.
Waves roll in with a silly splash,
As beach balls bounce with a joyful crash.

Shells tell tales of playful fish,
A dentist octopus grants a wish.
Flip-flops fly, caught in a breeze,
While laughter unfolds among palm trees.

Kites soar high, dancing with grace,
While seagulls glide, tracing their space.
A clam reads poems, quite absurd,
Filling the air with every word.

In this land of whirls and swirls,
Where summer fun and laughter twirls,
Every moment, a hasty dance,
In a place where humor finds its chance.

Secrets in the Mist of Morning

Whispers dance as dawn awakes,
Socks and sandals, oh the stakes!
Cereal floats like tiny boats,
Honey spills—better call the goats!

Jellybeans in coffee cups,
Sipping laughs from puppy pups,
Mist rolls in, the seagulls glide,
Waffles wobble on the side.

Bacon sings a crispy tune,
Sunshine pranks the waking moon.
Eggs are juggling, play it cool,
While toast is drawing in the pool!

Lost my hat—now it's a kite,
Chasing seagulls feels just right,
Tickled toes from ocean's spray,
Morning giggles lead the way.

Flowers Swaying in the Wind

Sunflowers gossip, petals tease,
Bumblebees whizzing with such ease.
Tulips twirl in twinkling light,
Dancing daisies take their flight.

Roses wear a fragrant grin,
Ferns in tuxedos, bright and thin.
A daffodil throws shade in fun,
While pansies laugh—this must be done!

Petals whisper fashion tips,
For garden parties and wild quips.
Lily pads start to do the slide,
Join the flowers, it's a ride!

Butterflies paint with colors bold,
Flirting with bees, that's how legends unfold.
With pollen glitters in the air,
Nature's jesters everywhere.

Horizons of Crystal Blue

Gumbo pots on sandy shores,
Seashells hide behind closed doors.
Fish flip-flop and try to chat,
While crabs play tag, imagine that!

Kites are soaring on a breeze,
Sailboats jockey, trying to please.
Napping turtles search for shade,
Polka-dots in sunbaked parade!

A clam pretends it's on a throne,
While dolphins dance with a blown cone.
Mango slices dripped in sun,
Ice cream's melting—oh, what fun!

Salted chips sing salty songs,
Laughing gulls play silly prongs.
Horizon winks, a visual feast,
Let's party now—a joyful beast!

Reflections on Ocean's Edge

Mirrors sparkle on the sand,
Crab walks in, demands a band.
Reflections giggle, waves do sway,
Seashells whisper, 'Come and play!'

Seagulls spin in loop-de-loops,
Shells parade in fancy groups.
Painting sunsets from the shore,
While flip-flops sing an ocean roar!

Tide pools hold a concert grand,
Peeking starfish wave their hand.
Jellyfish in disco lights,
Dancing under starry nights.

Splashing puddles catch the sun,
Water fights are just good fun.
Laughter echoes, life's a game,
At ocean's edge, we're all the same!

Brushstrokes of the Pacific

The sun paints smiles on the ocean,
Waves giggle, causing a commotion.
Fish wear sunglasses on their fins,
While crabs prance, showing off their sins.

Seagulls squawk in tuneful chatter,
While turtles dance, oh, what a clatter!
Palm trees sway with a casual grace,
They throw shade at the tourists' race.

Surfboards fly like overly eager kites,
Riding the waves, from day to nights.
Sandcastles crumble, laughter ignites,
As kids with shovels win epic fights.

And when the day blushes with hues,
Fishermen tell tales of their big blues.
Each sunset brings a comedic delight,
As we toast to sea life under starlight.

Gardens in the Mist of Dusk

At twilight, frogs tune their instruments,
While crickets hum in full consonants.
Flowers giggle, their petals in sync,
As bees wear hats and clink their drinks.

Misty shadows play hide and seek,
With fireflies flashing their little cheek.
A turtle hosts a tea party soirée,
While rabbits nap on scrapbooks of hay.

Laughter bubbles like a gentle stream,
In this garden, nothing's as it seems.
Gnomes in the corner snicker and scheme,
Planning a prank with a wild ice cream.

The stars blush as the moon joins in,
To watch the antics of a squirrel's grin.
In such a place, joy never lacks,
As magic unfolds in hilarious tracks.

Spirits of the Sea Breeze

Ghosts of sailors tell tall tales,
As mermaids giggle and hide their scales.
They spin yarns of 'what once was here,'
While dolphins drop hints, full of cheer.

The wind whispers secrets, oh so sweet,
Playing tag with everyone's feet.
Crabs host karaoke on the shells,
As the ocean's rhythm casts its spells.

Octopuses juggle on the shore,
While seahorses dance, begging for more.
Parrots crack jokes, perched high above,
In a colorful world, making us love.

As night falls with a wink and a sigh,
Stars twinkle back, lighting the sky.
In this quirky realm, each laugh afresh,
We savor the quirks, living life enmesh.

Celestial Reflections in the Lagoon

In the lagoon where dreams collide,
Moonbeams bounce, creating joyride.
Frogs wear costumes, hosting grand balls,
As the owls dance with their silvery thralls.

Fish with sunglasses swim in lines,
While turtles write weathered old signs.
The reeds are chatting, sharing wise cracks,
As fireflies leap, showing off their tracks.

Stars drop jokes like twinkling coins,
While the water sneezes, and the night joins.
Splashing laughter fills the whole space,
As the galaxy swirls at a comical pace.

In this haven of wonders profound,
Each ripple carries a laugh that's renowned.
With every moment, joy will bloom,
As the night wraps us in hilarity's room.

Lament of Distant Shores

Seagulls caw and dive for fries,
Tourists toss, much to our sighs.
Sand castles fall, like dreams at dawn,
Is it a beach? Or just a yawn?

Shells are treasures, or so they claim,
A crab nabs one and plays a game.
Flip flops flying, chaos reigns,
Who needs calm when fun remains?

Sand in sandwiches, grains in rice,
Every bite feels like a heist.
Pinching toes and chasing waves,
Life's a riddle no one braves.

Lemonade spills, sticky, oh dear,
An oddly shaped sunburn's our fear.
Yet laughter rings and joy ignites,
What a sight to behold on these nights!

Patterns of Light on Water

Reflections dance, a playful sight,
Fish wearing shades, oh what a plight!
The sunbeams giggle, skipping by,
Mermaids wave, they know why.

Ripples chuckle as rafts go past,
One tips over, and we all gasp!
The water swirls in a carefree spin,
As laughter bubbles, let the fun begin!

Drifting clouds draw silly shapes,
A boat's hat is swallowed by gapes.
The crabs join in with clacking jaws,
Applauding each of nature's flaws.

Castles built of laughter's foam,
Isn't this chaos a sweet home?
Shimmering views within this mirth,
Indeed, it's folly at its birth!

Threads of the Island Tapestry

Each wave whispers a secret tale,
Where surfboards glide and seagulls sail.
Palm trees sway with a goofy charm,
Tickling breezes that mean no harm.

Coconut hats wobble and bounce,
Surfers ride crests like a clown found.
A fish jumps up—what a surprise!
Emerging slapstick, a watery prize!

Island folks, parade of quirks,
Dance to rhythms, forget their works.
Shell necklaces and goofy grins,
Every hiccup's where fun begins!

With laughter a thread, we weave and mold,
An island's spirit, bright and bold.
This tapestry's made from joy's design,
Come join the jest, it's purely fine!

Sighs of the Evening Canvas

Twilight paints with hues so bright,
While fireflies play in whimsical flight.
Stars wink down, like they're in on it,
An artist's smirk that shall not quit.

Laughter spills from bonfire flames,
Marshmallows roasted, goofing names.
The moon-mischief stirs a laugh,
Beneath its glow, we lose the path.

Silly stories of ghosts and fate,
Are shared with giggles, oh it's great!
Sea turtles dance while shadows skip,
Around the embers, a joyous trip.

In this canvas, the night's embrace,
With echoes of laughter, takes its place.
Sigh, oh sigh, what a merry scene,
Here's to the night, and the laughter keen!

Driftwood Dreams and Ocean Glimmers

A coconut rolls down the street,
Dodging a flip-flop beat.
Seagulls squawk in a dance of cheer,
While crabs plot to commandeer.

Sandy toes and salty hair,
Flip-flops squeak with quite a flair.
Mango slices taste so sweet,
But sticky fingers—no retreat!

Here comes the ice cream truck so loud,
Chasing children, a lively crowd.
Sunburns hide beneath those hats,
As laughter blurs like playful chats.

Drifting dreams on a wave's smile,
Who knew fun could stretch a mile?
Waves crash with a joyous might,
As evening builds with twinkling light.

Harvest of Alight Reflections

Tomatoes ripe, the plants all giggle,
While watering cans dance and wiggle.
The garden blooms a vibrant scene,
With sunflowers that make frogs lean.

A pickle jar just rolled away,
While veggies prance, they lead the play.
Carrots hop with a sprightly tune,
While potatoes bask beneath the moon.

Butterflies host a garden show,
With blossoms dressed in petals' glow.
Lettuce makes a lovely crown,
As bees give all the gossip down.

The harvest yields a funny feast,
Where critters dance and cheers increase.
With laughter echoing in the night,
Nature's humor feels so right.

Essence of Salt and Sunshine

Under the sun, a picnic's set,
But ants have made a bold onset.
Sandwiches launch like a flying ace,
As seagulls join the wild race.

Lemonade spills with a splashing grin,
While laughter swirls, let the fun begin!
The blanket flaps like a tiny sail,
As kids giggle over a salt-smeared tale.

A frisbee whirls, then crashes wide,
Into the beach ball's sunny ride.
Sand castles rise, but tides conspire,
As waves play tricks, and kids retire.

At sunset's glow, the antics cease,
With jelly-sticky hands, we find peace.
Under starlit sky, dreams take flight,
As laughter lingers in the night.

Fragments of Paradise in the Wind

Tumbleweeds dance with glee and cheer,
While kites flutter, announcing they're here.
A beach ball bounces over the heads,
Creating chaos where laughter spreads.

Sandy critters plot their fun,
While chasing shadows, two kittens run.
Their tails up high, they leap and play,
Turning an ordinary day to ballet.

The waves whisper secrets bright,
As surfers dance on the edge of light.
Splashing rides and salty sighs,
Turn frowns to grins as joy complies.

Fragments of fun in the winds of fate,
With laughter shared, we congregate.
As sun dips low, horizons fade,
Chasing memories in the shade.

Laughter on the Lagoon's Edge

On the shore, we play and spin,
The crabs dance, wearing silly grins.
A parrot squawks a joke or two,
While fish swim by, all in a hue.

The turtles lay their heavy shells,
As seaweed tickles, oh it swells!
A sea slug laughs, a tale to tell,
In this bright place, all is so well.

We flip-flop through the sandy sand,
Discovering treasures, oh so grand.
With laughter ringing through the air,
We trip on waves, without a care.

A beach ball flies, it hits a shark,
He raises an eyebrow, gives a bark.
With giggles echoing on the tide,
Laughter flows like the ocean wide.

Tides That Sing in Softest Hues

Beneath the waves, a tune is played,
The fish all sway, in sunlit shade.
A dolphin flips, lets out a laugh,
While clams are humming in their half.

The starfish tap their quirky feet,
As jellyfish float, oh what a treat!
With colors bright, the tide does sing,
A cacophony of ocean bling.

A sea cucumber joins the show,
With wobbly moves, putting on flow.
Each wave that crashes brings a cheer,
In hues of laughter, oh my dear!

As shells applaud the concert grand,
The ocean's chorus takes a stand.
With all who play in waters blue,
We dance to rhythms, fresh and new.

Hummingbirds Over Coral Reefs

Tiny fliers, zipping by,
With glittering wings, oh my, oh my!
They sip the nectar, soft and sweet,
A buzzing band, a joyous fleet.

The corals chuckle, colors burst,
Encouraging birds, with quips rehearsed.
With every flutter, smiles appear,
In this bright realm, there's naught to fear.

A sea anemone wiggles tight,
Trying to grab a bird in flight.
The tiny hummer darts away,
While laughter echoes, bright as day.

Their dances quick, their laughter bold,
In underwater stories told.
While reefs rejoice in giggly cheer,
The hummingbirds just swoop and steer.

Serenade of the Evening Breeze

As sunsets paint the sky so wide,
The sea sighs softly, takes its ride.
With crickets chirping, joining in,
The breeze begins to laugh and spin.

A coconut drops, thuds on the ground,
As the palm trees sway, without a sound.
A hermit crab scuttles in delight,
In the warm hues of the fading light.

The sand shimmies, tickles our toes,
While seagulls croak in funny prose.
A beach party starts with clinks and clanks,
Giggling at tour boats filling pranks.

As stars burst forth in evening's glow,
The waves just giggle, ebb and flow.
With every whisper, giggles tease,
In the gentle serenade of the breeze.

Songs of the Mango Moon

Under the mango tree, a party of ants,
Who waltz to the rhythm, and take their chances.
They sip on sweet nectar, in mismatched pants,
While a lizard croons old love ballad dances.

A fruit flew past me, I thought it a hat,
But it turned out to be a fierce fruit bat!
We laughed 'til we cried, oh, what a chat,
As the moon giggled back, in a sparkling spat.

With coconuts floating like boats in the night,
We rode on the waves of our laughter, delight.
A crab joined the fun, with dancing so tight,
Even the stars twinkled in sheer, pure fright.

So here's to the night, and to friends far and near,
With mangoes and laughter, we conquer all fear.
Let's sing 'til the dawn, and sip madam beer,
In a world full of smiles, we'll keep it sincere.

Silhouettes in the Trade Winds

A parrot complains, 'These winds are too bold!
I lost my cool shades, now I'm feeling old!'
As the sun throws its rays, a sight to behold,
And the palm trees all dance, like a story retold.

The turtles decided to throw a big bash,
In the shallows they boogie, with shells that all clash.
While the fish pull a prank, with a splash and a crash,
They bubble beneath waves, like it's all just a flash.

We built castles from sand, so wobbly and grand,
Until the tide winked, and claimed all it planned.
With a laugh and a shout, we all took a stand,
To build new dreams, hand in hand on the strand.

So here's to the laughter, the dance and the cheer,
While the seagulls keep watch as we sip our cold beer.
With stories of old, that'll enter your ear,
We'll toast to the day, and make memories dear.

Caress of the Soft Sand

The grains of gold tickle our toes so well,
As we ponder if seashells could sing or could tell.
A crab strikes a pose, in his own little shell,
While fish throw a party, beneath waves they swell.

We spotted a dolphin, with moves so absurd,
It flipped like a pancake, now that's quite the bird!
We laughed 'til our sides began to feel stirred,
With a splash and a giggle, our worries deferred.

The sun set a stage, with colors galore,
As the waves choreographed dances from shore.
A treasure chest opened, we found so much more,
A sandcastle made of silliness, never a bore.

So here's to the soft sand, the whispers it brings,
With laughter and joy, oh how brightly it sings.
In the heart of the tropics, where fun never clings,
We'll cherish each moment, and the joy that it flings.

Melodies from a Sun-Kissed Isle

On the sun-kissed isle, where the coconuts grin,
A monkey's a DJ, let the party begin!
With beats made of laughter, and dances of spin,
We sway to the rhythm, as the day wears thin.

The pelicans strut, wearing shades oh so bright,
As the sun melts away, turning day into night.
A crab with a towel claims his sunbathing right,
While the fish play charades, what a joyful sight!

The old man in the hammock starts singing a tune,
While the stars start to twinkle, and shine like a balloon.
With a wave of his hand, he invites us to swoon,
Over fruit salad dreams served up with a spoon.

So lift up your drinks, let's toast to the fun,
With the laughter and memories, we've joyfully spun.
As the night gently falls, and all worries are done,
We'll dance 'til the dawn, with the warmth of the sun.

Comfort of the Solitary Shore

I sat alone on sands of gold,
Watching the waves, feeling quite bold.
A crab scuttled by, with a sideways dance,
I pondered if he had plans for romance.

The seagulls squawked, such a silly affair,
As I tried to relax in the sun-kissed air.
But they stole my chips, oh what a crime!
Perhaps I should snack on seaweed this time.

A lonely hermit, or so I believe,
Crafting sandcastles, I will not grieve.
Each tower a dream, each moat a laugh,
Though my dinner plans turn to a salty gaffe.

So here I remain, with the ocean's tune,
While clams play their shells like a jazz band's croon.
The sun sets low, and I start to snore,
Yet even in dreams, I'm still on the shore.

Chords of Nature's Symphony

The ocean sings, a cheerful song,
With fishy whispers where they belong.
A dolphin in shades of pink and blue,
Dances like it's got something to prove.

Waves crash like cymbals, oh what a sound,
As seaweed giggles, swaying around.
A starfish grins, its limbs all askew,
Waving hello, as if saying, "How do you do?"

The breeze tickles me, what a funny feel,
Like a feathered friend doing a cartwheel.
While crabs play the drums with shells in a row,
I can't help but laugh at the better show.

Nature's orchestra never needs a stage,
Every silly creature plays a sweet page.
With laughter and splashes, it's all so grand,
This symphony's magic, in this funny land.

Harmony Beneath the Starry Vega

Under the stars, the night feels alive,
With fireflies buzzing as they jive.
A turtle wearing spectacles, oh what a sight,
Reading the waves, lost in delight.

The moon peeks down, a curious face,
I wonder if it knows this magic place.
A fish wearing glasses starts to croon,
While waves tickle toes, like a friendly tune.

Crickets chirp, keeping time with glee,
While the sand crabs hop along with me.
Even the shells join in on the fun,
Jiving and dancing, oh they've just won!

So here in the night, with humor afloat,
As dreams twinkle bright on this silvery boat.
Laughter is hidden in bubbles and waves,
In this cosmic dance, my spirit braves.

Journeys in a Celestial Boat

In a boat made of clouds, I drift and glide,
With fishy crew and a starfish guide.
We sail through giggles on a foamy sea,
Riding the waves as wild as can be.

A seagull with flair takes lead as a steer,
Telling tales of adventure, we all want to hear.
The jellyfish dance, smoothing the ride,
While a crab tells jokes, filling hearts with pride.

With cotton candy skies and popcorn waves,
We cruise through the sunset, oh how it paves!
Each splash brings laughter, each swirl brings cheer,
In this whimsical journey, we have no fear.

As evening arrives and stars start to twinkle,
Our boat hums along, sharing a twinkle.
A pirate parrot begins to recite,
"Every sea's a treasure, beneath moonlit night!"

Whispers of the Turquoise Sea

Seagulls squawk in silly glee,
Chasing fish with clumsy spree.
The sun shines bright, a golden dime,
While crabs do their waltz, just in time.

Beach balls bounce like clowns in flight,
Kids giggle at the comical sight.
A coconut rolls, causing a stir,
As a dog dives in with a big, wet blur.

Their laughter sounds like waves at play,
In this wacky paradise all day.
Flip-flops flop with every step,
As the sand tickles like a playful pet.

Tanned tourists dance with wild flair,
While dancing crabs give quite a scare.
With clam shells clacking seriously,
They join the conga, wild and free.

Gentle Currents of the Tropical Dawn

Morning light spills through the trees,
Inviting all to share some cheese.
Parrots squawk a tune so strange,
As the rooster crows, 'It's time to change!'

Tropical fruits bounce in the mix,
Mangoes and papayas playing tricks.
A pineapple slips, it flies in the air,
Crash landing near a tourist's chair.

The hammock swings with a gentle droll,
As someone snores, losing control.
An iguana thinks it's quite the charmer,
Stealing a hat, oh what a drama!

With laughter echoing near the shore,
Even the crabs can't help but roar.
The sun rises high, chasing off snores,
As we munch on toast and look for more!

Echoes of Island Lullabies

Napping turtles dream of the race,
As waves rock gently, a soft embrace.
A parrot croaks a lullaby tune,
While a sleeping child snores at noon.

The ukulele strums a happy beat,
As a crab gives dance lessons on the heat.
Even the fish swim with a sway,
Counting stars like it's a play.

Palm trees sway with a giggling breeze,
Tickling the snoozers, oh what a tease!
A starfish grins on its cozy rock,
As waves tickle toes, a gentle knock.

The night brings whispers of amusing dreams,
In this land of laughter, nothing's as it seems.
Close your eyes, let the island sing,
Where funny creatures make your heart swing.

Dance of the Coastal Vines

Vines twist and turn with playful grace,
As critters scamper, quick in the race.
Mangoes dangle, ripe and round,
While monkeys leap and spin around.

The sun sets low, a fiery ball,
As vines decide to stretch and sprawl.
A toucan's beak joins the fray,
In a conga line, hip-hip-hooray!

Coconuts roll like a bowling spree,
As palm trees sway, oh what a sight to see!
The rhythm of nature starts to play,
As laughter fills the end of the day.

With every twist, there's joy in the air,
The vines are dancing without a care.
In this coastal paradise, oh what fun,
Where every leaf bursts out to run!

Serendipity Under the Stars

Under the sky, with a wink and a grin,
Laughter spills softly, where tales begin.
The crickets are chirping, they think they can sing,
While I chase my flip-flops, it's a silly thing.

Melodies weave from the twinkling light,
A glow from the moon makes the shadows take flight.
The starfish are gossiping, oh what a sight,
As I step on a jellyfish, yikes! What a fright!

Pineapple hats on, we dance with the breeze,
Caught in a whirl with a mountainside tease.
The food's falling down from a sky colored blue,
As we giggle and munch, in a wild, vibrant hue.

So let's raise a toast to the moon's foolish grin,
To the laughter that echoes where summertime's been.
With friends all around and the stars shining bright,
We'll dance till the dawn, under love's silly light.

Traces of Wings in the Twilight

Whispers of night as the sun starts to fade,
Seagulls are laughing, they've got it made.
I'm tangled in seaweed—what an awkward sight,
With my toes in the sand, giving in to delight.

A crab in a tuxedo takes a stroll on the shore,
Pinching my ankles, oh what a bore!
The shadows are playing a game of tag,
As I chase my poor hat; oh, what a drag!

The stars start to wink, and the fish tell a tale,
About floods and high tides, and a hungry whale.
Laughter erupts as a dolphin jumps high,
While I slip on a slick rock, who knew I could fly?

In the twilight's embrace, the mischief takes flight,
We dance with the flowers and sing to the night.
With giggles and fun, we let worries unwind,
Creating memories, silly and kind.

Lagoon's Gentle Murmur

Splashing in waters that giggle and play,
The fishes are mocking, oh what a day!
Palm trees are waving, as if to say hi,
While I trip on a turtle, who just scoffs and sighs.

Bubbles are popping, making silly sounds,
A crab does a cha-cha, as it shuffles around.
With coconuts rolling and pineapples fly,
I swear I could dance, if I only could try!

The lagoon sings sweetly, as dusk draws near,
But my dancing's a riot—oh dear, oh dear!
A fish gives a wink, and I laugh in surprise,
As I swerve like a starfish, in my sun hat disguise.

Cheers to the splashes and stories we weave,
In the lagoon's embrace, there's magic to believe.
With giggles and grins, we'll twirl through the night,
As laughter unrolls like a kite taking flight.

Moonsong Above the Oasis

Under the moon with a mischievous glow,
The lizards are dancing, oh look at them go!
Cacti wear hats like they're out for a ball,
But one tips right over, oh what a fall!

With shadows that chuckle as they twist and twirl,
A breeze keeps on teasing my hair in a swirl.
The sands start to giggle as I waddle by,
Trying to catch scents of hibiscus pie.

The stars are all winkers, playing tricks with their light,
As crickets recite poems, tales of the night.
With laughter erupting over silliness shared,
Who knew an oasis could be so unprepared?

So here's to the mishaps, the fun, and the cheer,
With the moon as our witness, we'll dance without fear.
Let's sing to the laughs, as we raise up a cheer,
In the heart of the night, where joy is sincere.

Sweet Embrace of Turquoise Waters

In the morning, the fish wear ties,
Splashing about with cheerful cries.
Crabs do the cha-cha on the shore,
While seagulls squabble, seeking more.

Coconuts roll like little brown balls,
Pineapples plot their fruity brawls.
Flip-flops dance with each awkward step,
The tourists waddle, hoping to prep.

Sunset paints the sky with glee,
As dolphins play peek-a-boo by the sea.
Mermaids giggle at the tourists' flops,
While the sandcastles melt like butter drops.

Evening falls with a twinkling wink,
As everyone gathers to laugh and drink.
In this paradise, time takes a pause,
Just don't step on the crabs or cause a cause.

Sunlit Portraits of Coastal Life

With hats too big and towels too small,
The sunbathers rise; they're having a ball.
Seashells chatter beneath the waves,
While sandmen strike their funniest poses like braves.

Beach volleyball turns into a mess,
As players tumble in sun-kissed distress.
Children giggle, chasing sand fleas,
Their laughter floats like a tropical breeze.

The ice cream melts, what a sticky plight,
As gulls swoop down – they're quite the sight.
Kites tangle like hairbrushes in a fight,
But who cares? It's all too bright!

Dusk arrives, the colors collide,
With flip-flops lost, there's nowhere to hide.
The beach life rolls on, a whimsical spree,
Join the commotion; it's wild and free!

Ocean's Call at Eventide

The waves giggle as they crash ashore,
A clam sashays, oh what a chore!
Fish hold a summit in their small school,
As seaweed floats like a green, groovy pool.

Sandy toes make for slippery slips,
With surfboards sailing on wild trips.
A crab disputes with a lazy star,
Over who's the best dancer from afar.

As sunset kisses the water's edge,
Laughter erupts - it's a fun pledge!
Catch a jellyfish having a ball,
While mermaids' giggles echo through it all.

With nightfall comes a twinkling glow,
As fireflies join the giggling show.
Together we laugh beneath the moon's sway,
In this ocean drama, let's dance and play!

A Tincture of Tropical Tides

Lemonade spills, a fruity delight,
As friends wear shades at noon's hungry height.
The parrots squawk in vivid array,
While flip-flops chatter like children at play.

A hammock sways with a melodious creak,
While tourists argue about sunburned cheeks.
Palm trees wave, tossing out high-fives,
As sun-kissed joy dances and thrives.

The waves make puns as they kiss the sand,
While a beach bum claims he'll start a band.
A coconut joins, beats a hollow drum,
Echoing laughter, oh what fun to come!

When night encroaches, it's a starlit spree,
With dancing shadows under the banyan tree.
Life's a tiki torch, bright and absurd,
In this tropical paradise, joy's never deferred!

www.ingramcontent.com/pod-product-compliance
Lightning Source LLC
Chambersburg PA
CBHW072130070526
44585CB00016B/1614